# Contents

# Prudence Wisdom Happiness light the way

Quoted By the Wealth and Wise

An Anthology of influential inspirational Thoughts

Compiled by Guiyana Saint Fleur

My words to you,

Do you want to know something you already know, and don't fully believe, just yet? By the end of this book, you will begin to believe wholly.

Your thoughts are powerfully working for you or against you depending on your character. Your thoughts patterns and word choices are the tools you need to build the life of desirable good. Yes, plain and simple, your thoughts hold power and how you think matters. What we think matters.

Your mind does numerous things. For instance, it is providing you with a reality of your own personal perspective of your experiences and beliefs.

Paramount; a significant source and space that is divinely connected to the source of infinity.

The mind is a place of thoughts, emotion reflection, and behavior coordination. I like to think of this grandeur place as our present; as it is the abode of words in its most intelligent form; energy creation.

Quoted by the wealth and the wise is a collection of guidance quotes positioned in a way to align you genuinely to everyday excellence and achievements through thoughts. Also, this book is great for those who seek a more prosperous mindset, and for those who enjoy channeling through the thoughts of wealthy wise people of good character ethics.

An anthology designed to create effective thought patterns that keep you on the path of virtuous distinction and triumph.

Created to gradually shift the way you think by simply upgrading your thoughts and releasing ineffective habitual thinking that may be mental roadblocks to your success.

With a gladden heart, I am here to tell you that this has been proven through various notable research. Similar to the research of the impact of a proper environment producing achievers and nobleness of character; the environment of the mind is just as important. To alter your physical environment, you must first enhance your mental environment, character ethics, and how the mind process thoughts and information.. After my own personal research and reflection, I have found this to be one of the most important keys to genuinely aligning with everyday joy, wholesomeness, accomplishments, well-being ascension, and wealth. Shift your thoughts accordingly to the appropriate terms of wealth and be of good character.

How do you do this? One method of achieving this is by adopting wealthy people's ways of thinking and processing information. Understanding how wise and wealthy people think and why they think the way they do.

Wealth thought formation is a key component of financial intelligence. These great thoughts formulated into quotes, were taken from prominent individuals who achieved high levels of excellence, monetary aggrandization and other forms of prestigious accomplishments that are worthy of high recognition. Because of their prosperous thinking process, good character ethics, and spiritual well-being, self-actualization and achievement were possible for them. What they say matters; these individuals hold significant value.

Quoted by the Wealth and Wise was orchestrated for the purpose of leading minds to think like rich and wise people; consistently thinking about important matters that are valuable for a meaningful beautiful healthy world, and worthwhile living. Advancing, through our own abilities, solving problems all the while, and bettering living.

Each Quote selected for this anthology was specifically chosen and written in an order designed to guide readers to understand the journey of wealth through thoughts.
These quotes will guide your inner mind to think in new ways in comparison to successful people. Exposing your brain to effective ways of thinking and perceiving things.

Reading this book will enhance your thinking formation system and give you an understanding of how you can create and dwell in useful thoughts that are empowering and ethical. The brain will then seek to process these quotes in a way that best suits you and your desires that you seek to bring fruition.

With your thoughts, harvest great measures of value; and create the wealth you desire virtuously within your reality, and your life consistently.

Believe what you already know, yes, it's true. You are becoming wealthier and wiser.

Allow this book to be a mental guide to your paradigm of wealth and lasting wisdom through quotes.

"Wealth is important", quoted by the Wealth and Wise.

Together, hand in hand, we rose.

# Part I: The Wealth Mindset

*Expanding our wealth favorably. Wise Mind.*

*Well-thee unto us all*

It's what I am. What? Prosperity.

“The money you make is a symbol of the value

you create.”

**Idowu Koyenikan**, International Acclaimed Organizational consultant and author

"Summit."

**Guiyana Saintfleur** b. 1993 Businesswoman, Author, Philosopher, Philanthropist, Theorist, Naturalist, Investor, and Author

"I am the head, not the tail. Above, not below. Destiny is obligated by universal laws to conceive to the demands of unwavering faith, and I believe that I am "

**Who I create myself to be, is the highest**

**good I can be.**

**Guiyana Saintfleur** b. 1993 Businesswoman, Author, Philosopher, Philanthropist, Theorist, Naturalist, Investor, and Author

*"You are what you do, not what you say you'll do."*

**Carl Gustav Jung**, 1875-1961 Early 20th Century Psychotherapist and Psychiatrist, creator of Analytic Psychology

**"Everything we want to do in life requires discipline. And like strength, flexibility, and endurance, it can be built over time.**

"**Laird Hamilton** b. 1964 American big-wave surfer, co-inventor of to-in surfing, and fashion/action- sports model and actor

"I feel healthy! I feel happy!

**W. Clement Stone**, 1902 – 2002 American businessman, Philanthropist, and New Thought self-help book Author.

"Earn with your mind, not your time."

**Naval Ravikant**, b. 1974 Indian- American Entrepreneur and investor; Co-founder, chairman and former CEO of AngelList.

"Look at yourself as a Sovereignty. Think Sovereignty. Feel Sovereignty. Become Sovereignty. Stay Royal, Sovereignty loyalty."

Inner-Voice

“I am Healthy, happy, and whole.”

**Louise Hay** 1926 - 2017 American Motivational Author, Model, and founder of Hay House

"Persuasion, indeed, is a kind of force. It consists in showing a person the consequences of his actions. It is, in a word, force applied through the mind. "

**James Fitzjames Stephen**, 1829 -1894 Philosopher, writer, English Lawyer, and Judge

"Rich people believe "I create my life."

**T Harv Eker**, b. 1954 Author, Businessman, and Wealth Motivational Speaker

"I will arise one day and make a believer of all those who doubted me. I will love with no fear. I will boldly attack the things that scare me. They will not stop me on my destiny."

Queendom Comes

"I have a lot to be thankful for. I am healthy, happy and I am loved."

**Reba McEntire**, b. 1955 American Country Singer, Actress, and Business Woman

**Start where you are, with what you have.**

**Make something of it.**

**George Washington Carver** 1864-1943 Scientist and Educator

"You become what you believe, not what you think or what you want."

**Oprah Winfrey** b. 1954 American Talk Show Host, Television producer, actress, and author, and philanthropist

"Wealth is the ability to fully experience life."

**Henry David Thoreau**, 1817 - 1862 American Author, Naturalist, and Philosopher

Learn to do the common things

uncommonly well.

**George Washington Carver** 1864-1943 Scientist and Educator

"It is our collective and individual responsibility… To preserve and tend to the world which we all live."

Dalai Lama

"The liberation of the African Mind, Body, and Spirit can only be achieved through the use of an African centered value system that makes the study of the successes and failures of the past the highest priority."

Anthony T. Browder Cultural Historian, Author, publisher, artist, and educational consultant.

"Your opinion of yourself is your most important viewpoint. You are infinitely greater than you think you are."

**Neville Goddard** 1905 - 1972 Inspirer, Speaker, Bajan writer, and Mystic

"Reputation is the key to success. "

**SriLi Ka Shing**, b. 1928 Hong Kong Business Magnate, Investor, and Philanthropist

***I've always believed that if you put in the work,***

***the results will come.***

**Michael Jordan** b. 1963 Former professional basketball player and American businessman

"Don't practice until you get it right, practice until you can't get it wrong."

**Michael Jordan** b. 1963 Former professional basketball player and American businessman

I am loving and loyal to myself.

Inner Voice

"Believe in yourself and have confidence that you can compete against all odds. Have a vision of what you'd like to accomplish and be able to articulate that vision."

**Robert Louis Johnson** b. 1946 Co-founder of BET, American entrepreneur, philanthropist, media magnate, executive, and investor [First black American Billionaire].

"Formal education will make you a living; self-education will make you a fortune."

**Emanuel James Rohn** (Jim Rohns), 1930 -2009 American Entrepreneur, Author, Motivational Speaker

"The greatest discovery of all time is that a person can change his future by merely changing his attitude."

**Oprah Winfrey** b. 1954 American Talk Show Host, Television producer, actress, and author, and philanthropist

"You are already that which you want to be, and your refusal to believe this is the only reason you do not see it."

**Neville Goddard** 1905 - 1972 Inspirer, Speaker, Bajan writer, and Mystic

"Healthy Happy days! When you' re in alignment with yourself, it allows you to intentionally choose what you allow into your life."

The Voices of the Universe

"What we really want to do is what we are really meant to do. When we do what we are meant to do, money comes to us, doors open for us, we feel useful, and the work we do feels like play to us."

**Julia Cameron**, b. 1948 American Teacher, Author, Artist, Poet, Playwright, Novelist, Filmmaker, Pigeon Fancier, Composer, and Journalist

"Money doesn't fall out of the sky. We had a business plan, an extraordinary proposal, and it was the right timing."

**Sheila CJohnson** b.1949 Co-founder of BET, CEO of Salamander Hotels and Resorts, American billionaire businesswoman

***"The world is run by those who show up."***

**Robert Louis Johnson** b. 1946 Co-founder of BET, American entrepreneur, philanthropist, media magnate, executive, and investor [First black American Billionaire].

"The only real security that a man will have in this world is a reserve of knowledge, experience, and ability."

**Henry Ford**, 1863 – 1947 American industrialist, business magnate, founder of the Ford Motor Company

*Take action! An inch of movement will bring you closer to your goals than a mile of action.*

**Steve Maraboli** *b. 1975* *Author, Speaker, Inspirer*

## Part II: The Drive

*With our actions, progress, scale, we achieve*

*our goals.*

Prosperity is the norm for us.

*Do you want to know who you are? Don't ask. Act! Action will delineate and define you.*

**Thomas Jefferson** *b. 1743 – 1826 American Statesman, Planter, Lawyer, architect, philosopher, primary author of the Declaration of Independence, and third president of the United States.*

*Success seems to be connected with action. Successful people keep moving. They make mistakes but don't quit.*

**Conrad Hilton** b. 1987 - 1979 American businessman founded Hilton Hotels chain.

"The choices you make in your life will make your life. Choose wisely."

**Michael Josephson** b. 1942 Notable Author, Former Law Professor, Founder of Nonprofit Joseph and Edna Josephson Institute of Ethics

"My mission in life is not merely to survive, but to thrive; and to do so with some passion, some compassion, some humor, and some style."

**Maya Angelou** b. 1928- 2014 Memorable American Memoirist, Author, Poet, and Civil Activist

"When you truly maintain alkaline-forming foods in your body, you will maintain excellent health."

**Alfredo Darrington Bowman 'Legendary Dr. Sebi'** b. 1933 - 2016 Herbalist healer, Dependable Truth-Teller, Herbs and Plant-Based Alkaline Body Supporter

"It is the food that you eat that would reconnect you with the energies of life, and then words are unnecessary because you could see. You're connected."

**Alfredo Darrington Bowman 'Legendary Dr. Sebi'** b. 1933 - 2016 Herbalist healer, Dependable Truth-Teller, Herbs and Plant-Based Alkaline Body Supporter

*You don't have to be great to start, but you do have to start to be great.*

**Hilary Hinton 'Zig Ziglar'** *b. 1926 – 2012 Author, Motivational speaker, and Salesman*

*Small deeds done are better than great deeds planned.*

**Ralph Peirre LaCock 'Peter Marshall'** *b. 1926 Former game show host, television and radio personality, actor, and singer*

"I am removing any plaque from the system; I am removing inflammation. That is the basis of all disease.

I live with eu-ease."

Inner voice

*There are only two rules for being successful.*

*One, figure out exactly what you want to do,*

*and two, do it.*

*Mario Cuomo b. 1932 – 2015 American Lawyer and Politician, New York's 52nd Governor.*

All transformation begins with an intense, burning desire to be transformed. The first step in the 'renewing of the mind' is desire. You must want to be different [and intend to be] before you can begin to change yourself. Then you must make your future dream a present fact. You do this by assuming the feeling of your wish fulfilled. By desiring to be other than what you are, you can create an ideal of the person you want to be and assume that you are already that person. If this assumption is persisted in until it becomes your dominant feeling, the attainment of your ideal is inevitable.

The world is a mirror, forever reflecting what you are doing, within yourself.

**Neville Goddard** 1905 - 1972 Inspirer, Speaker, Bajan writer, and Mystic

"Get the fundamentals down and the level of

everything you do will rise."

**Michael Jordan** b. 1963 Former professional basketball player and American businessman

*"Do it. Do it right. Do it right now."*

**Spencer W. Kimball,** 1895 - 1985 Business, Civic, and Religious Leader

"Everything begins moving in the direction of what has your attention."

**Esther (Weaver) Hicks** b. 1974 American inspirational speaker, author.

**"Be honest about where you are in the process. Not just your role. Be honest about your abilities. Are they growing? Will what got you here get you there? If not, what are you prepared and excited to do to fill the gap?"**

Janice Bryant Howroyd b 1952 Entrepreneur, business owner, author, and founder and CEO of The ActOne Group the largest privately held, minority-woman-owned personnel company founded in the U.S.

**"Passion is energy. Feel the power that comes from focusing on what excites you."**

**Oprah Winfrey** b. 1954 American Talk Show Host, Television producer, actress, and author, and philanthropist

"In the Journey to success, tenacity of purpose is supreme. "

**Aliko Dangote** b. 1957 Nigerian Business Magnate, Industrial Conglomerate, African Billionaire

"Get going. Move forward. Aim High. Plan a takeoff. Don't just sit on the runway and hope someone will come along and push the airplane. It simply won't happen. Change your attitude and gain some altitude. Believe me, you'll love it up here."

**Donald Trump** b. 1946 Politician, Businessman, America 45th and 47th President

**"IF YOU ARE CONSCIOUS, YOU ARE BLESSED."**

**Alfredo Darrington Bowman 'Legendary Dr. Sebi'** b. 1933 – 2016 Herbalist healer, Dependable Truth-Teller, Herbs and Plant-Based Alkaline Body Supporter

"You have to diversify to grow. I'm not afraid to take risks and falls."

**Sheila CJohnson** b.1949 Co-founder of BET, CEO of Salamander Hotels and Resorts, American billionaire businesswoman

"Sometimes I'm having so much fun, I have to pinch myself to see if I'm dreaming."

Innervoice

"I'm cashing in on the excitement of making a difference in the world."

**David Steward**, b. 1951 Businessman, Chairman and founder of World Wide Technology (One of the Largest African-American Owned businesses in America)

"To do meaningful work is to contribute – to create value in society."

**Charles de Ganahl Koch** b. 1935 American Billionaire businessman, Co-owner, chairman, and chief executive officer of Koch Industries

"I'm proud of myself, I like the way I'm made."

**Freida Pinto** b. 1984 Indian Actress and Spokesmodel

"Endeavor to work as hard as possible to attain a new aim with each day that comes by. Don't go to bed until you have achieved something productive."

**Aliko Dangote** b. 1957 Nigerian Business Magnate, Industrial Conglomerate, African Billionaire

"I want to see what happens if I don' t give up."

Inner Voice

"People are all the same but you and I, we're not like them. So to say that we'll both stay,"

**Robert M Drake** American poet, novelist and visual artist

***"You've got to get up every morning with determination if you're going to go to bed with satisfaction."***

**George Lorimer** 1867 – 1937 American journalist, Estates owner, author, and publisher.

"The opportunity is in the problem. The moment I see a problem, I immediately begin to think about the opportunities that can be created by trying to solve it."

**Strive Masiyiwa** b. 1961 Zimbabwean billionaire businessman and philanthropist.

"Thinking opens the doors to our minds and makes us receptive to the very idea of broadening our horizons and learning new things."

**Alaklja Folorunsho** b. 1951 Nigerian billionaire businesswoman and philanthropist.

"In whatever you do, strive to be the best at it. "

**Aliko Dangote** b. 1957 Nigerian Business Magnate, Industrial Conglomerate, African Billionaire

"Change your conception of yourself and you will automatically change the world in which you live. Do not try to change people; they are only messengers telling you who you are. Revalue yourself and they will confirm the change."

**Neville Goddard** 1905 - 1972 Inspirer, Speaker, Bajan writer, and Mystic

"A truly wise person uses few words; a person with understanding is even-tempered."

**Proverbs 17:27**

*"Surround yourself with only people who are going to lift you higher. "*

**Oprah Winfrey** b. 1954 American Talk Show Host, Television producer, actress, and author, and philanthropist

"Every morning when I wake up, I make up my mind to solve as many problems, before returning home. "

**Aliko Dangote** b. 1957 Nigerian Business Magnate, Industrial Conglomerate, African Billionaire

"While education and talent are extremely important to attaining success, nothing can replace persistence and determination."

**Suzanne Shank** b. 1952 Notable Businesswoman, Wallstreet Expert, and Empowerment leader

"I know who I am. I know what I can and can't do. I know what I will and won't do. I know what I'm capable of and I don't agree to do things that I don't think I can pull off. "

**Dolly Parton** b. 1946 Country Singer-songwriter, Actress, and Businesswoman.

"Think with the thinkers and discover ideas that mold who you are. Smile at strangers and make friends that last a life-time. Laugh with friends and let those memories power your heart. Travel with travelers and explore a life beyond your imagination. Love only one and grow old with your bestfriend. Let these things bring fire to your soul. So when you look back at your life, you'll have no regrets and you can leave this place better than you found it."

**Robert M Drake** American poet, novelist and visual artist

"In the journey of an entrepreneur, the most important thing is self-belief and the ability to convert that belief into reality."

**Mukesh Ambani**, b. 1957 Wealthy Indian Business magnate, chairman, the largest shareholder of Reliance industries Ltd

"Don't kill the competition. Competition is healthy for businesses. It keeps you the entrepreneur on your toes."

**Aliko Dangote** b. 1957 Nigerian Business Magnate, Industrial Conglomerate, African Billionaire

“I love investing my time, money, and energy into excellent valuable contributions; and enjoying our world. I show this through my thoughts, words, and actions.”

**Guiyana Saintfleur** b. 1993 Businesswoman, Author, Philanthropist, Theorist, Naturalist, Investor, and Author

**“When I look at this company, I envision a billion-dollar business, and that’s how it’s run.”**

**David Steward** b. 1951 Businessman, Chairman and founder of World Wide Technology (One of the Largest African-American Owned businesses in America)

"A good businessman must have nose for business the same way a journalist has nose for news. Once your eyes, ears, nose, heart and brain are trained on business, you sniff business opportunities everywhere. "

**Orji Uzor Kalu** b. 1960 Nigerian politician, Senator, and Businessman

“Everybody resonates differently.

And everybody comes with a good

message afforded in a different

way.”

**Alfredo Darrington Bowman 'Legendary Dr. Sebi'** b. 1933 – 2016 Herbalist healer, Dependable Truth-Teller, Herbs and Plant-Based Alkaline Body Supporter

"We must be mindful of the fact that every image we see on television or film, every publication that we read, and every sound we hear on CD, radio and media has been carefully crafted by specialists and is designed to elicit a specific response from the audience. Black people must be particularly aware of the negative images of us that have been manufactured in the media over the years. Such media manipulation continues today. In reality, television, film, and radio are powerful electronic forces that saturate the mind and body with sights and sounds that influence psychological, emotional, and spiritual well-being. Its effects can be controlled by acknowledging its existence and learning to neutralize the negative influences it projects."

**Anthony T. Browder** Cultural Historian, Author, publisher, artist, and educational consultant.

“We can transcend the script of a pre-defined story, and pave the way for the future that we design. We just need to tap that power, that conviction, that determination within us.”

**Robert F Smith** b. 1962 Businessman and Philanthropist, American Billionaire

## Part III: Prosperity Accomplished Gratitude

Love, Knowledge, Comprehension, and

Wisdom

are life's greatest gifts. Thank you life.

"It's not the employer who pays the wages. Employers only handle the money. It's the customer who pays the wages."

**Henry Ford.** 1863 – 1947 American industrialist, business magnate, founder of the Ford Motor Company

"When you have made it in life, you must give back to those who made you. "

**Aliko Dangote** b. 1957 Nigerian Business Magnate, Industrial Conglomerate, African Billionaire

*"Today be thankful and think how rich you are. Your family is priceless, your time is gold, and your health is wealth. "*

**Hilary Hinton 'Zig Ziglar'** *b. 1926 – 2012 Author, Motivational speaker, and Salesman*

"The one thing you want to do is to love, and that love should begin with you. Once you love you, you love the whole world."

**Alfredo Darrington Bowman 'Legendary Dr. Sebi'** b. 1933 – 2016 Herbalist healer, Dependable Truth-Teller, Herbs and Plant-Based Alkaline Body Supporter

"It's good to have money and the things that money can buy, but it's good, too, to check up once in a while and make sure that you haven't lost the things that money can't buy."

**George Lorimer** 1867 – 1937 American journalist, Estates owner, author, and publisher.

"There are so many different ways to make your family. I'm just super-grateful to have my children."

**Emma Clare Thynn,** b. 1986 Marchioness of Bath, British socialite, and fashion model

"Having a baby is the best thing in the world for married stable couples and adults."

**Emma Clare Thynn** b. 1986 Marchioness of Bath, British socialite, and fashion model

"We are creating multi-cultural billion-dollar business owner mindsets with honorable character ethics."

**Guiyana Saintfleur** b. 1993 Businesswoman, Author, Philanthropist, Theorist, Naturalist, Investor, Author

. "A leader is a visionary who successfully carries others along to achieve a particular goal, within a specific time frame."

**Alakija Folorunsho** b. 1951 Nigerian billionaire businesswoman and philanthropist.

"We are natural healers, Eliminate the

mucus and you eliminate the disease."

**Alfredo Darrington Bowman 'Legendary Dr. Sebi'** b. 1933 - 2016 Herbalist healer, Dependable Truth-Teller, Herbs and Plant-Based Alkaline Body Supporter

"It's cool to be healthy."

**Dick Gregory** 1932 - 2017 American comedian, Civil rights leader, Author, and Vegetarian activist

"You're made of elements. Take the time to learn the foods with high element properties in order to save your health and your body."

**Alfredo Darrington Bowman 'Legendary Dr. Sebi'** b. 1933 – 2016 Herbalist healer, Dependable Truth-Teller, Herbs and Plant-Based Alkaline Body Supporter

"There's a God force inside of you that gives you

a will to live."

**Dick Gregory** 1932 - 2017 American comedian, Civil rights leader, Author, and Vegetarian activist

"I told as much of my life as I could to encourage people to encourage others to get to where they should be., where they want to be."

**Alakija Folorunsho** b. 1951 Nigerian billionaire businesswoman and philanthropist

*"When I tune into my beautiful self, I get happiness. Everything in the universe belongs to me."*

**Dick Gregory** 1932 - 2017 American comedian, Civil rights leader, Author, and Vegetarian activist

Create the highest, grandest vision possible for your life, because you become what you believe.

**Oprah Winfrey** b. 1954 American Talk Show Host, Television producer, actress, and author, and philanthropist

I say to you brothers and sisters. If nothing else we do, let us be tolerant of each other – and share LOVE."

**Alfredo Darrington Bowman 'Legendary Dr. Sebi'** b. 1933 – 2016 Herbalist healer, Dependable Truth-Teller, Herbs and Plant-Based Alkaline Body Supporter

## Summary

The mind is a powerful thing, a powerful tool. A powerful source. Thoughts are prominent, divine. In a world of unlimited data, what information unlocks the doors that you want open; our virtuous desires? The door that holds your thoughts perceiving the details all around you and the words you speak. Knowing is the first step; processing the information for efficaciousness is the next. Following is our ability to retain the information, the knowledge for the purpose of gaining the data primarily, and continually building upon it, expanding objectively favorably. What you believe, with good virtue make it true.

The way the mind process and think are grand experiences.

Secret told, your thoughts hold power, use it wisely.

"I always knew I was destined for greatness."

**Oprah Winfrey** b. 1954 American Talk Show Host, Television producer, actress, and author, and philanthropist

You and I. We are

Grateful

www.ingramcontent.com/pod-product-compliance
Ingram Content Group UK Ltd.
Pitfield, Milton Keynes, MK11 3LW, UK
UKHW061826190726
13853UKWH00009B/2447